10-MINUTE
DISHES

Editor:
Valerie Ferguson

LORENZ BOOKS

Contents

Introduction

Every day produces greater demands on our time and one of the first things sacrificed to life on the run is enjoyable and nutritious meals. This collection of recipes is the perfect solution for busy people who don't want to live on unhealthy snacks and ready-made food. All the dishes can be prepared and cooked in 10 minutes and some of them take even less time. There are recipes for all tastes, courses and occasions, whether you want a quick and easy starter for a dinner party so that you can lavish care and time on the main course; you are late home from work and the family is screaming for food; or you are simply tired and hungry and don't want to spend much time in the kitchen.

The introduction includes useful advice on stocking your store cupboard with 'short-cut' ingredients to make food preparation easier. Dishes that combine quick-cooking fresh ingredients with ready-made or store cupboard items are a good compromise and will still be full of flavour and nutrients.

Fast food can still be good food. These recipes all demonstrate that you don't have to be chained to a hot stove for flavour-packed, nourishing and attractive meals.

The Store Cupboard

Your store cupboard should be the backbone of your kitchen. Stock it sensibly and you'll always have the wherewithal to make a tasty, satisfying meal. Check use-by dates on stored items regularly and avoid overstocking.

Canned Goods

Some canned products are very useful for quick cooking. Chickpeas, cannellini beans, green lentils, haricot (navy) beans, red kidney beans and butter (lima) beans survive the canning process well. Wash in cold running water and drain before use. Canned artichoke hearts have a mild, sweet flavour and are great for adding to stir-fries, salads, risottos and pizzas. Additional useful items to include are ratatouille and pimientos.

Grains

Both brown and white easy-cook rice are available. Alternatively, when you have time to cook rice, prepare an extra batch and freeze it. There are other quick-cook grains available, too, including couscous and polenta.

Nuts

Buy nuts in small quantities and store in a dry place or freeze. Almonds, cashews, peanuts, pecans, pine nuts and walnuts are all useful ingredients.

Oils

Groundnut, sunflower and vegetable oils are bland tasting and will not mask delicate flavours, so they can be used for all cooking, including deep frying. Olive oil cannot be used for deep frying, but will suit most purposes. Extra virgin olive oil is more expensive and is best kept for salads. Sesame oil and chilli oil are useful flavourings, used in small quantities in stir-fries.

Pasta

While fresh pasta is best, both for flavour and for speed of cooking, the dried product is a valuable store cupboard ingredient. Spaghetti, noodles (Italian and Oriental) and shapes are all useful.

Sauces & Flavourings

A range of sauces provides an easy way to add extra flavour to a dish without spending any more time. Soy sauce can be added at the end of cooking and extra offered at the table. Black bean sauce is a thick aromatic sauce, used in stir-fries. Tahini paste, made from ground sesame seeds, is used in Middle-Eastern cooking. Pesto, made from basil and pine nuts, is used in Italian cooking. Ready-made mayonnaise and salad dressings vary in quality: the best are often the most expensive.

Spices & Herbs

Buy spices and dried herbs in small quantities and store in a cool, dark place. A useful collection of spices would include ground cumin, coriander, turmeric, garam masala and chilli for hot, spicy dishes, while cinnamon, cardamom and cloves add a sweet, fragrant flavour to savoury and sweet dishes.

Herbs such as thyme, rosemary, sage, basil and marjoram retain their flavour when dried.

Above: A selection of useful ingredients for your store cupboard.

Tomato Products

Canned tomatoes are essential and a wide range is available, such as whole or chopped, plain or with herbs, spices or other flavourings. Sun-dried tomatoes are sweet and intensely flavoured. They are available in packets or steeped in oil in jars. The oil can also be used for additional flavouring. Tomato purée (paste) is a concentrated paste sold in cans, jars or tubes. There is also a version made from sun-dried tomatoes. Passata, a thick, smooth sauce made from sieved (strained) tomatoes, is mainly used in Italian cookery.

Menu Planner

If you are entertaining guests and want to expand your 10-minute main course into a quick three-course meal, here are some suggestions for delicious, well-balanced combinations on different themes.

Menu 1
A Taste of the Exotic

Thai-style Sweetcorn Soup

Menu 2
A Summer Lunch Party

Asparagus with Tarragon Butter

Glazed Chicken with Cashew Nuts

Salmon with Tropical Fruit Salsa

Quick Apricot Blender Whip

Ice Cream Strawberry Shortcake

Menu 3
A Winter Dinner Party

Parma Ham with Mango Slices

Veal Escalopes with Tarragon

Orange Yogurt Brûlées

Menu 4
A Vegetarian Meal

Chickpea Purée

Multi-mushroom Stroganoff

Brazilian Coffee Bananas

Thai-style Sweetcorn Soup

This is an easy soup, made in minutes. If you are using frozen prawns (shrimp), thaw them first before adding to the soup.

Serves 4

INGREDIENTS
2.5 ml/½ tsp sesame or sunflower oil
2 spring onions (scallions), thinly sliced
1 garlic clove, crushed
600 ml/1 pint/2½ cups chicken stock
425 g/15 oz can cream-style sweetcorn
225 g/8 oz/1¼ cups cooked,
    peeled prawns (shrimp)
5 ml/1 tsp green chilli paste or
    chilli sauce (optional)
salt and freshly ground black pepper
fresh coriander (cilantro) leaves, to garnish

1 Heat the oil in a large, heavy pan and sauté the onions and crushed garlic over a medium heat for 1 minute, until the onions and garlic are softened, but not browned.

2 Stir in the chicken stock, cream-style sweetcorn, prawns and chilli paste or sauce, if using.

3 Bring the soup to the boil, stirring occasionally. Season to taste, then serve at once, sprinkled with fresh coriander leaves to garnish.

Borscht

This soup is a simplified version of the classic eastern European dish and
is prepared in a fraction of the time.

Serves 4

INGREDIENTS
30 ml/2 tbsp vegetable oil
1 medium onion, halved and sliced
5 ml/1 tsp caraway seeds
finely grated rind of ½ orange
250 g/9 oz/1⅔ cups cooked beetroot (beet),
   grated
1.2 litres/2 pints/5 cups beef stock
400 g/14 oz can butter (lima) beans, drained
15 ml/1 tbsp wine vinegar
60 ml/4 tbsp soured cream
salt and freshly ground black pepper
60 ml/4 tbsp fresh parsley, to garnish

1 Heat the oil in a large saucepan
and cook the sliced onion, caraway
seeds and orange rind until soft, but
not coloured.

2 Add the grated, cooked beetroot,
stock, drained butter beans and wine
vinegar. Cover and simmer for a
further 8 minutes. Season well with
salt and pepper.

3 Divide the soup among four bowls,
add a spoonful of soured cream to
each and scatter with chopped fresh
parsley. Serve piping hot.

Chicken Stellette Soup

Cooked chicken breasts are available from most supermarkets or you can use leftover roast chicken for this speedy soup.

Serves 4–6

INGREDIENTS
900 ml/1½ pints/3¾ cups
   chicken stock
1 bay leaf
225 g/8 oz/3¼ cups button (white)
   mushrooms, sliced
4 spring onions (scallions), sliced
50 g/2 oz/½ cup soup
   pasta (stellette)
115 g/4 oz cooked chicken breast
150 ml/¼ pint/⅔ cup dry
   white wine
15 ml/1 tbsp chopped
   fresh parsley
salt and freshly ground
   black pepper

1 Put the stock and bay leaf into a medium pan and bring to the boil over a medium heat.

2 Add the sliced button mushrooms and sliced spring onions to the stock and stir to mix.

3 Add the pasta to the pan. Season to taste with salt and ground black pepper, then cover and simmer over a low heat for 7–8 minutes.

4 Meanwhile, remove the skin from the cooked chicken and slice thinly. Add the chicken, wine and parsley to the soup and heat through. Serve the soup immediately.

VARIATION: Vegetarians could use vegetable stock and substitute the chicken with cubed, marinated and fried tofu.

Melon & Grapefruit Cocktail

This pretty, colourful starter can be made in minutes.

Serves 4

INGREDIENTS
1 small Galia or Ogen melon
1 small Charentais melon
2 pink grapefruit
45 ml/3 tbsp orange juice
60 ml/4 tbsp red vermouth
seeds from ½ pomegranate
fresh mint sprigs, to decorate

1 Halve the melons lengthways and scoop out all the seeds. Cut into wedges and remove the skins, then cut across into large bite-size pieces.

2 Using a small, sharp knife, cut the peel and pith from the grapefruit. Holding the fruit over a bowl to catch the juice, cut between the grapefruit membranes to release the segments. Set aside the grapefruit segments.

3 Stir the orange juice and vermouth into the bowl containing the grapefruit juice. Arrange the fruit on four plates. Spoon over the dressing, scatter with pomegranate, garnish with mint. Serve.

Right: Melon & Grapefruit Cocktail (top);
Parma Ham with Mango Slices

Parma Ham with Mango Slices

This light, elegant starter is amazingly simple to prepare.

Serves 4

INGREDIENTS
16 slices Parma ham
1 ripe mango
freshly ground black pepper
fresh flat leaf parsley sprigs, to garnish

1 Separate the Parma ham slices and arrange four on each of four individual plates, crumpling the ham slightly to give a decorative effect.

2 Cut the mango into three thick slices around the stone, then slice the flesh and discard the stone. Neatly cut away the skin from each slice.

3 Arrange the mango slices among the ham. Grind over some black pepper and serve garnished with flat leaf parsley sprigs.

Guacamole

This popular Mexican dish is meant to have a chunky texture. Serve it the traditional way, with corn chips.

Serves 4

INGREDIENTS

2 ripe avocados, peeled and stoned
2 tomatoes, peeled, seeded and chopped
6 spring onions (scallions), finely chopped
1–2 chillies, seeded and finely chopped
30 ml/2 tbsp fresh lime or lemon juice
15 ml/1 tbsp chopped fresh coriander
   (cilantro) and extra sprigs, to garnish
salt and freshly ground black pepper
corn chips, to serve

1 Put the avocado halves into a large bowl and mash them with a fork.

2 Add the remaining ingredients. Mix well and season according to taste. Serve garnished with fresh coriander and corn chips.

COOK'S TIP: To save even more time, substitute 1.5–2.5 ml/¼–½ tsp chilli powder for the fresh chillies.

Chickpea Purée

What would once have been a time-consuming appetizer can now be made in moments using a food processor.

Serves 4

INGREDIENTS
400 g/14 oz can chickpeas, drained
2 small garlic cloves, halved
60 ml/4 tbsp fresh
    parsley leaves
60 ml/4 tbsp olive oil, plus extra, to garnish
30 ml/2 tbsp lemon juice
salt and freshly ground
    black pepper
fresh flat leaf parsley, to garnish

1 Process the chickpeas, garlic and parsley in a food processor until finely chopped. With the motor running, slowly pour in the olive oil and lemon juice to make a thick purée.

2 Add salt and pepper to taste. Spoon the purée into a bowl, cover and chill until ready to serve, garnished with extra olive oil and a sprig of parsley.

VARIATION: For a change, try making this tapas dish with other canned beans, such as cannellini.

Hot Tomato & Mozzarella Salad

A quick, easy starter with a Mediterranean flavour.

Serves 4

INGREDIENTS
450 g/1 lb plum tomatoes, sliced
225 g/8 oz Mozzarella cheese, sliced
1 red onion, finely chopped
4–6 pieces sun-dried tomatoes in oil, drained
  and chopped
60 ml/4 tbsp olive oil
5 ml/1 tsp red wine vinegar
2.5 ml/½ tsp Dijon mustard
60 ml/4 tbsp chopped fresh mixed herbs,
  such as basil, parsley, oregano and chives
salt and freshly ground black pepper
fresh herbs, to garnish

1 Arrange the sliced tomatoes and Mozzarella in circles in four individual shallow flameproof dishes.

2 Scatter the chopped onion and sun-dried tomatoes over the top.

3 Whisk together the olive oil, vinegar, mustard, chopped herbs and seasoning. Pour over the salads.

4 Place the salads under a hot grill for 4–5 minutes, until the Mozzarella starts to melt. Grind the black pepper over and serve garnished with fresh herbs.

Asparagus with Tarragon Butter

This simple and elegant starter involves little effort.

Serves 4

INGREDIENTS
500 g/1¼ lb fresh asparagus
115 g/4 oz/ 8 tbsp butter
30 ml/2 tbsp chopped fresh tarragon
15 ml/1 tbsp chopped fresh parsley
grated rind of ½ lemon
15 ml/1 tbsp lemon juice
salt and freshly ground black pepper

1 Trim the woody ends from the asparagus spears, then tie them into four equal bundles.

2 Place the bundles of asparagus in a large frying pan with about 2.5 cm/ 1 in boiling water. Cover and cook for about 6–8 minutes, until tender but still firm. Drain well and discard the strings.

3 Meanwhile, melt the butter in a small pan. Add the tarragon, parsley, lemon rind and juice and seasoning.

4 Arrange the asparagus on four warmed plates. Pour the hot tarragon butter over and serve.

Right: Hot Tomato & Mozzarella Salad (top); Asparagus with Tarragon Butter

Fried Monkfish with Tapenade

Fish lends itself to fast cooking, and cutting it into small pieces speeds up the process even more.

Serves 3–4

INGREDIENTS
450 g/1 lb fresh
    monkfish fillet
30 ml/2 tbsp olive oil
450 g/1 lb jar tapenade
salt and freshly ground
    black pepper
chopped fresh parsley and diced
    red pepper, to garnish

2 Heat the olive oil in a heavy-based frying pan and fry the fish on one side for 2 minutes. Turn the fish over and cook for a further 1 minute.

3 Place a generous spoonful of tapenade in the centre of each of four serving plates and arrange the fish around each mound. Sprinkle with fresh parsley and diced red pepper and serve.

1 Cut the monkfish fillets into rounds about 2.5 cm/1 in thick. Season with salt and pepper.

COOK'S TIP: Tapenade is a Provençal olive paste flavoured with capers, anchovies, basil and garlic.

VARIATIONS: Monkfish is ideal for the busy cook and it can also be grilled or poached. Serve with tomato sauce, either prepared in advance and frozen, or use a jar of sauce instead. Or, try monkfish kebabs with peppers, mushrooms and courgettes (zucchini), brushed with oil and grilled or barbecued.

Cajun-style Cod

Using a very high heat ensures that the fish cooks so quickly that there is no time for the spices to burn.

Serves 4

INGREDIENTS

4 cod steaks, each weighing
about 175 g/6 oz
30 ml/2 tbsp natural (plain) yogurt
15 ml/1 tbsp lime or
lemon juice
1 garlic clove, crushed
5 ml/1 tsp ground cumin
5 ml/1 tsp paprika
5 ml/1 tsp mustard powder
2.5 ml/½ tsp cayenne pepper
2.5 ml/½ tsp dried thyme
2.5 ml/½ tsp dried oregano
salt
15 ml/1 tbsp vegetable oil
halved lemon slices, to garnish
new potatoes and a mixed salad,
to serve

2 Mix together the crushed garlic clove, spices, herbs and salt. Coat both sides of the fish with the seasoning mix, rubbing in well.

3 Brush a ridged griddle with the oil, or heat it in a frying pan. When it is very hot, add the fish and cook over a high heat for 4 minutes, or until the underside is well browned.

VARIATION: If preferred, griddle the cod using salt and pepper instead of spices. Serve with a pat of anchovy butter: blend half a can of anchovies with 50 g/2 oz/¼ cup butter.

1 Pat the cod steaks dry on kitchen paper. Mix together the yogurt and lime or lemon juice and brush this mixture lightly over both sides of the fish.

4 Turn over and cook for a further 3 minutes, or until the steaks have cooked through. Serve accompanied by new potatoes and a mixed salad and garnished with lemon.

COOK'S TIP: This recipe works equally well with any firm-fleshed fish, such as swordfish, shark, tuna, hake or halibut.

Salmon with Tropical Fruit Salsa

A colourful fresh fruit salsa, prepared in minutes, turns plain grilled salmon into an exotic dish.

Serves 4

INGREDIENTS
4 salmon steaks or fillets,
  about 175 g/6 oz each
finely grated rind and juice
  of 1 lime
1 small, ripe mango
1 small, ripe papaya
1 red chilli
45 ml/3 tbsp chopped
  fresh coriander (cilantro)
salt and freshly ground
  black pepper
coriander (cilantro) sprigs, to garnish

1 Place the salmon in a wide dish and sprinkle over half the lime rind and juice. Season with salt and pepper.

2 Cut the mango in half, cutting either side of the stone, and then remove the stone. Finely chop the mango flesh.

3 Halve the papaya, scoop out the seeds and remove the peel, then chop the flesh finely.

4 Cut the chilli in half lengthways. For a milder flavour, remove the seeds, or leave the seeds in to make the salsa hot and spicy. Finely chop the chilli.

5 Combine the mango, papaya, chilli and coriander in a bowl and stir in the remaining lime rind and juice. Season to taste with salt and pepper.

6 Cook the salmon on a hot barbecue or under a preheated grill for 5 minutes, turning once. Serve with the salsa and garnish with coriander.

COOK'S TIP: If fresh red chillies are not available, use about 2.5 ml/ ½ tsp of chilli paste from a jar, or add a dash of chilli sauce.

Pan-fried Sole

Simple cooking and seasoning suits this delicate fish, so any more elaborate preparation would just be a waste of time.

Serves 2

INGREDIENTS
350 g/12 oz skinless
   sole fillets
120 ml/4 fl oz/½ cup milk
50 g/2 oz/½ cup plain (all-purpose) flour
15 ml/1 tbsp vegetable oil
15 g/½ oz/1 tbsp butter
15 ml/1 tbsp chopped
   fresh parsley
salt and freshly ground
   black pepper
lemon wedges, to garnish

1 Rinse the fish fillets and gently pat dry using absorbent kitchen paper.

2 Put the milk into a shallow dish about the same size as a fish fillet. Put the flour in another shallow dish and season with salt and pepper.

3 Heat the oil in a large frying pan over a medium-high heat and add the butter. Dip a fish fillet into the milk, then into the flour, turning to coat well, then shake off the excess.

4 Put the coated fillets into the pan in a single layer. Fry the fish gently, turning once, for 3–4 minutes, until lightly browned. Sprinkle the fish with chopped parsley and serve garnished with wedges of lemon.

VARIATION: Dover sole has the most flavour, but lemon sole is also superb.

Buckwheat Noodles with Smoked Trout

This Eastern-influenced dish looks and tastes as though it takes at least twice as much time and effort than it really does.

Serves 4

INGREDIENTS
350 g/12 oz buckwheat noodles
30 ml/2 tbsp vegetable oil
115 g/4 oz/1¾ cups fresh shiitake
    mushrooms, quartered
2 garlic cloves, finely chopped
15 ml/1 tbsp grated fresh
    root ginger
225 g/8 oz pak choi
1 spring onion (scallion), finely
    sliced diagonally
15 ml/1 tbsp dark sesame oil
30 ml/2 tbsp mirin or medium sherry
30 ml/2 tbsp soy sauce
2 smoked trout, skinned and boned
salt and freshly ground black pepper
30 ml/2 tbsp coriander (cilantro) leaves and
    10 ml/2 tsp sesame seeds, toasted,
    to garnish

3 Drain the noodles and add them to the mushroom mixture with the spring onion, sesame oil, mirin or sherry and soy sauce. Toss and season with salt and pepper to taste.

4 Break the smoked trout into bite-size pieces. Arrange the noodle and mushroom mixture on individual serving plates. Place the smoked trout on top of the noodles.

1 Cook the buckwheat noodles in a pan of boiling water for about 7–10 minutes, or until just tender, following the directions on the packet.

2 Meanwhile heat the oil in a large frying pan. Add the shiitake mushrooms and sauté over a medium heat for 3 minutes. Add the garlic, ginger and pak choi and continue to sauté for 2 minutes.

5 Garnish the noodles with coriander leaves and toasted sesame seeds and serve them immediately.

Sautéed Scallops

With little preparation and cooking time, this classic French dish is ideal after a hard day's work.

Serves 2

INGREDIENTS
450 g/1 lb shelled scallops
25 g/1 oz/2 tbsp butter
30 ml/2 tbsp dry white vermouth
15 ml/1 tbsp finely chopped fresh parsley
salt and freshly ground black pepper

1 Rinse the scallops under cold running water to remove any sand or grit and pat dry using kitchen paper. Season them lightly with salt and black pepper.

2 In a frying pan large enough to hold the scallops in one layer, heat half the butter until it begins to colour. Sauté the scallops for 3–5 minutes, turning, until golden brown on both sides and just firm to the touch. Remove to a serving platter and cover to keep warm.

3 Add the vermouth to the hot frying pan, swirl in the remaining butter, add the chopped parsley and pour the sauce over the scallops. Serve immediately.

Right: Sautéed Scallops (top);
Garlicky Seafood

Garlicky Seafood

This Mediterranean seafood dish is speedily prepared using a cooking method typical in Provence.

Serves 2–4

INGREDIENTS
6 large shelled scallops
6–8 large raw prawns (shrimp), peeled
plain (all-purpose) flour, for dusting
30–45 ml/2–3 tbsp olive oil
1 garlic clove, finely chopped
15 ml/1 tbsp chopped fresh basil
30–45 ml/2–3 tbsp lemon juice
salt and freshly ground black pepper

1 Rinse the scallops under cold running water to remove any sand or grit. Pat them dry using kitchen paper and cut in half crossways. Season the scallops and prawns with salt and pepper and dust lightly with flour, shaking off excess.

2 Heat the oil in a large frying pan over a high heat and add the scallops and prawns.

3 Reduce the heat to medium-high and cook for 2 minutes, then turn the scallops and prawns and add the garlic and basil, shaking the pan to distribute them evenly. Cook for a further 2 minutes until golden and just firm to the touch. Sprinkle over the lemon juice and toss to blend. Serve.

Chicken with Olives

Chicken breasts or turkey, veal or pork escalopes may be flattened for quick and even cooking.

Serves 4

INGREDIENTS
4 skinless boneless chicken breasts
(about 150–175 g/5–6 oz each)
1.5 ml/¼ tsp cayenne pepper
75–105 ml/5–7 tbsp extra virgin
olive oil
1 garlic clove, finely chopped
16–24 stoned black olives
6 ripe plum tomatoes, roughly chopped
small handful fresh basil leaves, shredded
salt

1 Carefully remove the fillets (the long finger-shaped muscle on the back of each chicken breast) and reserve for another use.

2 Place each chicken breast between two sheets of clear film (plastic wrap) and pound with the flat side of a meat mallet or roll out with a rolling pin to flatten the meat to about 1 cm/½ in thick. Season with salt and the cayenne pepper.

3 Heat 45–60 ml/3–4 tbsp of the olive oil in a large, heavy frying pan over a medium-high heat. Add the chicken breasts and cook for 4–5 minutes, until golden brown and just cooked through, turning once. Transfer to warmed serving plates and keep warm.

4 Wipe out the frying pan and return to the heat. Add another 30–45 ml/ 2–3 tbsp of olive oil and fry the garlic for 1 minute, until golden and fragrant. Stir in the olives, cook for another minute, then stir in the tomatoes. Stir in the shredded basil then spoon the sauce over the chicken and serve at once.

COOK'S TIP: If the tomato skins are at all tough, remove them by scoring the base of each tomato with a knife, then plunging them into boiling water for 45 seconds. The skin should simply peel off.

Chicken Chow Mein

The Chinese virtually invented fast food when they designed the wok and discovered stir-frying.

Serves 4

INGREDIENTS
350 g/12 oz noodles
225 g/8 oz skinless, boneless
· chicken breasts
45 ml/3 tbsp soy sauce
15 ml/1 tbsp Chinese rice wine or
    dry sherry
15 ml/1 tbsp dark sesame oil
60 ml/4 tbsp vegetable oil
2 garlic cloves, finely chopped
50 g/2 oz mangetouts (snow peas),
    topped and tailed
115 g/4 oz/½ cup beansprouts
50 g/2 oz ham, finely shredded
4 spring onions (scallions), finely chopped
salt and freshly ground
    black pepper

2 Slice the chicken into fine shreds about 5 cm/2 in long. Place in a bowl and add 10 ml/2 tsp of the soy sauce, the rice wine or sherry and sesame oil.

3 Heat half the vegetable oil in a wok over a high heat. When it starts smoking, add the chicken mixture. Stir-fry for 2 minutes, then transfer to a plate and keep it hot.

1 Cook the noodles in a pan of boiling water until tender. Drain, rinse under cold water and drain well once again. Set aside.

4 Wipe the wok clean and heat the remaining oil. Stir in the garlic, mangetouts, beansprouts and shredded ham, stir-fry for another minute and add the noodles.

5 Continue to stir-fry until the noodles are heated through. Add the remaining soy sauce to taste and season with salt and pepper. Return the chicken and any juices to the wok, add the spring onions and give the mixture a final stir. Serve at once.

Glazed Chicken with Cashew Nuts

Slicing the ingredients into similarly sized pieces is the secret to fast and even cooking for this flavoursome chicken dish.

Serves 4

INGREDIENTS
75 g/3 oz/½ cup cashew nuts
1 red (bell) pepper
450 g/1 lb skinless, boneless
   chicken breasts
45 ml/3 tbsp groundnut oil
4 garlic cloves, finely chopped
30 ml/2 tbsp Chinese rice wine or
   dry sherry
45 ml/3 tbsp hoisin sauce
10 ml/2 tsp sesame oil
5–6 spring onions (scallions), green parts
   only, cut into 2.5 cm/1 in lengths

3 Heat the oil in a preheated wok. Add the chopped garlic and let it sizzle for a few seconds. Add the pepper and chicken strips and stir-fry for 2 minutes.

1 Heat the wok until hot, add the cashew nuts and stir-fry over a low to medium heat for 1–2 minutes, until golden brown. Remove and set aside.

2 Halve and seed the pepper. Slice the pepper and chicken into finger-length strips.

4 Add the rice wine or sherry and hoisin sauce. Continue to stir-fry until the chicken is tender and all the ingredients are evenly glazed.

VARIATION: Use blanched almonds instead of cashew nuts, if you prefer.

5 Stir in the sesame oil, toasted cashew nuts and spring onion tips. Serve immediately.

Pork in Sweet & Sour Sauce

The time spent slicing and flattening the pork will be adequately repaid by the speed with which it cooks to crisp perfection.

Serves 2

INGREDIENTS
1 whole pork fillet (tenderloin),
    about 350 g/12 oz
25 ml/1½ tbsp plain (all-purpose) flour
30 ml/2 tbsp olive oil
250 ml/8 fl oz/1 cup dry white wine
30 ml/2 tbsp white wine vinegar
10 ml/2 tsp sugar
15 ml/1 tbsp mixed peppercorns,
    coarsely ground
salt and freshly ground
    black pepper
broad (fava) beans tossed with grilled bacon,
    to serve (optional)

2 Spread out the flour in a shallow bowl. Season with salt and pepper and coat the meat.

3 Heat 15 ml/1 tbsp of the oil in a wide, heavy-based pan or frying pan and add the pork. Fry over a medium to high heat for 2–3 minutes on each side until crispy and tender. Remove with a fish slice and set aside.

COOK'S TIP: Grind the mixed peppercorns in a pepper grinder or crush them with a mortar and pestle.

1 Cut the pork fillet diagonally into thin slices using a sharp knife. Place the slices between two sheets of clear film (plastic wrap) and pound lightly with a rolling pin or meat mallet to flatten them evenly.

4 Mix the wine, wine vinegar and sugar in a jug (pitcher). Pour into the pan and stir vigorously over a high heat until reduced. Stir in the peppercorns and return the pork to the pan. Spoon the sauce over the pork until it is evenly coated and heated through. Serve immediately with broad beans and bacon, if liked.

Stuffed Naan

This is a good way to provide a nourishing dish when the children are hungry and can hardly wait to eat.

Serves 4

INGREDIENTS
115 g/4 oz/1 cup minced (ground) beef
115 g/4 oz/1 cup pork sausagemeat
    (bulk sausage)
5 ml/1 tsp mixed
    dried herbs
15 ml/1 tbsp brown sauce
4 mini naan breads
60 ml/4 tbsp mango chutney
salt and freshly ground
    black pepper
green salad, to serve

2 Add the sausagemeat and herbs and season well with salt and pepper. Stir in the brown sauce and mix to combine thoroughly. Preheat the grill.

1 Place the minced beef in a medium bowl and break it up thoroughly using a fork.

VARIATION: If preferred, the patties could be put inside a burger bun or pitta bread, and the mango relish could be replaced with a tomato or corn relish.

3 Bring the mixture together with your hands and form into four patties. Grill under a medium heat for 8 minutes, turning once.

4 Towards the end of the cooking time, place the naan breads under the grill for 2–3 minutes. Split with a knife and place the patties and chutney inside. Serve with a crisp green salad.

Grilled Steak Salad

Combining fresh and ready-made ingredients saves time without any loss of flavour, texture, variety and nutrients.

Serves 4

INGREDIENTS
4 sirloin or rump steaks, each
    weighing 175 g/6 oz
1 escarole lettuce
1 bunch watercress
4 tomatoes, quartered
4 large gherkins, sliced
4 spring onions (scallions), sliced
4 canned artichoke hearts, halved
175 g/6 oz/2½ cups button (white)
    mushrooms, sliced
12 green olives
120 ml/4 fl oz/½ cup
    French dressing
salt and freshly ground
    black pepper

2 Meanwhile, wash the salad leaves and spin dry. Combine with the remainder of the ingredients (except the steak) and toss with the dressing.

3 Divide the salad among four plates. Slice each steak diagonally and position over the salad. Season with salt and serve.

1 Season the steaks with pepper. Cook the steaks under a moderate grill for 6–8 minutes, turning once, until medium-rare. Cover and leave to rest in a warm place.

COOK'S TIPS: Avoid buying steak with any gristle as this is a sign of old and tough meat.
    Salt added during cooking draws out the juices from the steak.

Pan-fried Veal Chops

Basil complements veal perfectly.

Serves 2

INGREDIENTS
olive oil, for brushing
2 veal loin chops, 2.5 cm/1 in thick (about
   225 g/8 oz each)
25 g/1 oz/2 tbsp butter, softened
15 ml/1 tbsp Dijon mustard
15 ml/1 tbsp chopped fresh basil
salt and freshly ground black pepper

1 Lightly oil a heavy frying pan or griddle. Set over a high heat until very hot, but not smoking. Brush both sides of each chop with a little oil and season with salt.

2 Place the veal chops on the pan or griddle and reduce the heat to medium. Cook for 4–5 minutes, then turn the chops and cook for a further 3–4 minutes, until done as preferred (medium-rare meat will be slightly soft when pressed, medium meat will be springy, and well-done firm).

3 Meanwhile, make the basil butter. Cream the butter with the mustard and chopped basil in a small bowl, then season with pepper. Transfer the chops to warmed serving plates, top each one with half the basil butter and serve.

Veal Escalopes with Tarragon

A quick and elegant dish.

Serves 4

INGREDIENTS
4 veal escalopes (about 115–150 g/4–5 oz
   each) flattened to 5 mm/¼ in thick
15 g/½ oz/1 tbsp butter
30 ml/2 tbsp brandy
250 ml/8 fl oz/1 cup chicken or
   beef stock
15 ml/1 tbsp chopped fresh tarragon
salt and freshly ground black pepper
fresh tarragon sprigs, to garnish

1 Season the escalopes to taste. Melt the butter in a large frying pan over a medium-high heat. Add the meat in one layer and cook for 1½–2 minutes, turning once. (It should be lightly browned, but must not be overcooked.) Transfer to a platter and cover to keep warm.

2 Add the brandy to the pan, pour in the stock and bring to the boil. Add the tarragon and continue boiling until the liquid is reduced by half.

3 Return the veal to the pan with any accumulated juices and heat through. Serve immediately, garnished with tarragon sprigs.

Right: Pan-fried Veal Chops (top);
Veal Escalopes with Tarragon

Calf's Liver with Balsamic Vinegar

Thin slices of tender calf's liver will cook the moment they hit the pan, and the vinegar sauce can be made in moments.

Serves 2

INGREDIENTS
15 ml/1 tbsp plain (all-purpose) flour
2.5 ml/½ tsp finely chopped fresh sage
4 thin slices of calf's liver,
   cut into serving pieces
45 ml/3 tbsp olive oil
25 g/1 oz/2 tbsp butter
2 small red onions, sliced and
   separated into rings
150 ml/¼ pint/⅔ cup dry
   white wine
45 ml/3 tbsp balsamic vinegar
pinch of sugar
salt and freshly ground black pepper
fresh sage sprigs, to garnish
green beans sprinkled with browned
   breadcrumbs, to serve (optional)

1 Spread out the flour in a shallow bowl. Season it with the sage and plenty of salt and pepper. Turn the liver in the flour until well coated.

2 Heat 30 ml/2 tbsp of the oil with half of the butter in a wide, heavy-based pan or frying pan until foaming. Add the onion rings and cook gently, stirring frequently, for about 5 minutes, until softened but not coloured. Remove and set aside.

3 Heat the remaining oil and butter in the pan until foaming, add the liver and cook over medium heat for 2–3 minutes on each side. (Make sure the liver is not overcooked, because it quickly turns tough. It should be slightly underdone and pink.) Transfer to heated plates and keep hot.

4 Add the wine and vinegar to the pan, then stir to mix with the pan juices and any sediment. Add the onions and sugar and heat through, stirring. Spoon the sauce over the liver, garnish with sage sprigs and serve at once with the green beans, if liked.

Soufflé Omelette

Easy, tasty, fast and made from fresh, simple ingredients – what more could you want when hungry and short of time?

Serves 1

INGREDIENTS
2 eggs, separated
30 ml/2 tbsp water
15 ml/1 tbsp chopped
   fresh coriander (cilantro)
7.5 ml/1½ tsp olive oil
30 ml/2 tbsp mango chutney
25 g/1 oz/¼ cup Jarlsberg
   cheese, grated
salt and freshly ground
   black pepper
mixed salad leaves, to serve

2 Whisk the egg whites until stiff, but not dry, and gently fold into the egg yolk mixture.

1 Using a fork, beat the egg yolks together with the cold water and coriander. Season to taste with salt and pepper.

COOK'S TIP: A light hand is essential to the success of this dish. Do not overmix the whisked egg whites into the yolks or the mixture will be heavy.

3 Heat the oil in a frying pan, pour in the egg mixture and reduce the heat. Do not stir. Cook until the omelette becomes puffy and golden brown on the underside (carefully lift one edge with a palette knife to check).

4 Spoon on the chutney and sprinkle on the Jarlsberg. Fold over and slide on to a warm plate. Eat immediately with the salad. (If preferred, before adding the chutney and cheese, place the pan under a hot grill to set the top.)

Multi-mushroom Stroganoff

Soured cream or crème fraîche makes a wonderful sauce.

Serves 3–4

INGREDIENTS
45 ml/3 tbsp olive oil
450 g/1 lb/6½ cups mushrooms (including ceps, shiitakes or oysters), sliced
3 spring onions (scallions), sliced
2 garlic cloves, crushed
30 ml/2 tbsp dry sherry or vermouth
300 ml/½ pint/1¼ cups soured cream or crème fraîche
15 ml/1 tbsp fresh marjoram or thyme leaves, chopped
fresh parsley, chopped
salt and freshly ground black pepper
rice or pasta, to serve

1 Heat the oil in a large frying pan and fry the mushrooms gently, stirring them occasionally, until they are softened and just cooked.

2 Add the spring onions, garlic and sherry or vermouth and cook for a minute more. Season well.

3 Stir in the soured cream or crème fraîche and heat to just below boiling. Stir in the marjoram or thyme, then scatter over the parsley. Serve immediately with rice or pasta.

Speedy Bean & Pesto Pasta

This is a perfectly balanced and utterly delicious dish.

Serves 4

INGREDIENTS
225 g/8 oz/2 cups dried pasta shapes
pinch of freshly grated nutmeg
30 ml/2 tbsp extra virgin olive oil
400 g/14 oz can butter (lima) beans, drained
45 ml/3 tbsp pesto sauce
150 ml/¼ pint/⅔ cup single cream
salt and freshly ground black pepper
fresh basil sprigs, to garnish
45 ml/3 tbsp pine nuts, to serve
freshly grated Parmesan cheese, to serve (optional)

1 Boil the pasta until tender, but still firm to the bite, then drain, leaving it a little wet. Return the pasta to the pan, season, and stir in the nutmeg and oil.

2 Meanwhile, heat the beans in a pan with the pesto and cream, stirring constantly until the mixture begins to simmer. Toss the beans and pesto into the cooked pasta and mix well. Serve in bowls topped with pine nuts and grated Parmesan, if wished. Garnish with basil.

Right: Multi-mushroom Stroganoff (top); Speedy Bean & Pesto Pasta

French Bread Pizzas with Artichokes

Crunchy French bread makes an ideal base for these quick pizzas which are perfect for when you come home from work.

Serves 4

INGREDIENTS
15 ml/1 tbsp sunflower oil
1 onion, chopped
1 green (bell) pepper, seeded and chopped
200 g/7 oz can chopped tomatoes
15 ml/1 tbsp tomato purée (paste)
½ French stick
400 g/14 oz can artichoke
    hearts, drained
115 g/4 oz Mozzarella cheese, sliced
15 ml/1 tbsp poppy seeds
salt and freshly ground
    black pepper

1 Heat the oil in a frying pan. Add the chopped onion and pepper and cook until just softened.

2 Stir in the chopped tomatoes and tomato purée. Cook for 2 minutes. Remove from the heat and season with salt and pepper to taste.

3 Meanwhile, cut the piece of French stick in half lengthways. Cut each half in four to give eight pieces in all.

4 Preheat the grill. Spoon a little of the pepper and tomato mixture over each piece of bread.

5 Slice the drained artichoke hearts. Arrange them on top of the pepper and tomato mixture. Cover with the Mozzarella slices and sprinkle with the poppy seeds.

6 Arrange the French bread pizzas on a grill rack and grill for 5 minutes, until the cheese melts and is beginning to brown. Serve at once.

VARIATION: The artichokes could be replaced with a can of drained asparagus tips.

Balti Stir-fried Vegetables with Cashew Nuts

Serves 4

INGREDIENTS
2 medium carrots
1 medium red (bell) pepper, seeded
1 medium green (bell) pepper, seeded
2 courgettes (zucchini)
115 g/4 oz/¾ cup green beans
1 medium bunch spring onions (scallions)
15 ml/1 tbsp virgin olive oil
4–6 curry leaves
2.5 ml/½ tsp white cumin seeds
4 dried red chillies
10–12 cashew nuts
5 ml/1 tsp salt
30 ml/2 tbsp lemon juice
fresh mint leaves, to garnish

1 Prepare the vegetables: cut the carrots, peppers and courgettes into matchsticks, halve the beans and chop the spring onions. Set aside.

2 Heat the oil in a non-stick wok or frying pan and fry the curry leaves, cumin seeds and dried chillies for about 1 minute.

3 Add the vegetables and nuts and stir gently. Add the salt and lemon juice. Continue to stir and cook for about 3 minutes.

4 Transfer to a warmed serving dish and serve garnished with mint.

Fried Noodles with Beansprouts

The wok's sloping sides assist the method of stir-frying.

Serves 2

INGREDIENTS
115 g/4 oz dried egg noodles
60 ml/4 tbsp vegetable oil
1 small onion, chopped
2.5 cm/1 in piece of fresh root
    ginger, grated
2 garlic cloves, crushed
175 g/6 oz young asparagus
    spears, trimmed
115 g/4 oz/½ cup beansprouts
4 spring onions (scallions), sliced
45 ml/3 tbsp soy sauce
salt and freshly ground
    black pepper

1 Cook the noodles in boiling salted water for 2–3 minutes, until just tender. Drain. Toss in 30 ml/2 tbsp of the oil.

2 Meanwhile, heat the remaining oil in a wok or frying pan until hot. Add the onion, ginger and garlic and stir-fry for 2–3 minutes. Add the asparagus and stir-fry for a further 2–3 minutes.

3 Add the noodles and beansprouts and stir-fry over a medium heat for 2 minutes. Stir in the spring onions and soy sauce. Season to taste. Stir-fry for 1 minute, then serve.

Quick Apricot Blender Whip

This just has to be one of the quickest desserts you could make, and also one of the prettiest. The Grand Marnier gives it a delightful lift.

Serves 4

INGREDIENTS
400 g/14 oz can apricot halves
  in juice
15 ml/1 tbsp Grand Marnier or brandy
175 ml/6 fl oz/¾ cup Greek (US strained
  plain) yogurt
30 ml/2 tbsp flaked almonds

1 Drain the juice from the apricots and place the fruit and liqueur in a blender or food processor. Process the apricots until smooth.

2 Spoon the fruit purée and yogurt in alternate spoonfuls into four tall glasses or glass dishes, swirling them together slightly to give a marbled effect.

3 Lightly toast the almonds until they are golden. Let them cool slightly and then sprinkle them on top.

VARIATION: If preferred, you could omit the Grand Marnier and add a little of the fruit juice from the can instead.

Brazilian Coffee Bananas

Rich, lavish and sinful-looking, this very easy-to-make dessert takes only about two minutes to prepare and serve.

Serves 4

INGREDIENTS
4 small ripe bananas
15 ml/1 tbsp instant coffee granules
15 ml/1 tbsp hot water
30 ml/2 tbsp muscovado (molasses) sugar
250 ml/8 fl oz/1 cup Greek (US strained plain) yogurt
15 ml/1 tbsp toasted flaked (sliced) almonds

1 Peel and slice 1 banana and mash the remaining 3 with a fork. Dissolve the coffee in the hot water and stir into the mashed bananas.

2 Spoon a little of the mashed banana mixture into four serving dishes and sprinkle with sugar. Top with a spoonful of yogurt, then repeat until all the ingredients are used up.

3 Swirl the last layer of yogurt for a marbled effect. Finish with a few banana slices and toasted flaked almonds. Serve cold.

VARIATION: For a special occasion, add a dash of dark rum or brandy to the bananas for extra richness.

Ice Cream Strawberry Shortcake

No one would ever guess that this dashing dessert can be assembled from ready-made ingredients in just a few minutes.

Serves 4

INGREDIENTS
3 x 15 cm/6 in sponge flan cases, or
    shortbreads
675 g/1½ lb/6 cups hulled
    fresh strawberries
1.2 litres/2 pints/5 cups vanilla or
    strawberry ice cream
icing (confectioner's) sugar, for dusting

2 Halve the hulled strawberries (if time), reserving 3 for decoration. Place one-third of the ice cream and strawberries on to a sponge flan case or shortbread.

1 If using sponge flan cases, carefully trim the raised edges with a sharp serrated knife.

COOK'S TIP: Don't worry if the shortbread falls apart when you cut into it. Messy cakes are best. Ice Cream Strawberry Shortcake can be assembled up to 1 hour in advance and kept in the freezer without spoiling the fruit.

3 Cover with a second sponge or shortbread and make a second layer of ice cream and strawberries in the same way. Finish with the last sponge or shortbread, and place the remaining ice cream and strawberries on top. Dust with icing sugar and serve.

Orange Yogurt Brûlées

This is a fast-track version of the classic, but time-consuming dessert. It is also much easier to prepare.

Serves 4

INGREDIENTS

2 medium-size oranges
150 ml/¼ pint/⅔ cup
   Greek (US strained plain) yogurt
50 ml/2 fl oz/¼ cup crème fraîche
45 ml/3 tbsp golden
   caster (superfine) sugar
30 ml/2 tbsp light muscovado
   (brown) sugar

3 Mix together the golden caster and light muscovado sugars and sprinkle them evenly over the top of the yogurt and crème fraîche mixture in each dish.

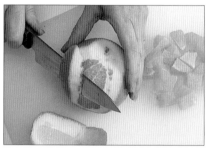

1 Preheat the grill. With a sharp knife, cut away all the peel and white pith from the oranges and chop the fruit. (If you have time, you can cut the segments away from the membrane before you chop them.)

2 Place the fruit in the bottom of four individual flameproof dishes. Mix together the Greek yogurt and crème fraîche and spoon the mixture over the oranges.

4 Place the dishes under a very hot grill for 3–4 minutes, or until the sugar melts and turns to a rich golden brown. Serve warm or cold.

COOK'S TIP: For a lighter version, use 250 ml/8 fl oz/1 cup low-fat natural (plain) yogurt instead of the Greek yogurt and crème fraîche.

Chilled Ricotta & Marsala Pudding

This rich dessert is easy to make and, as it can be made up to 24 hours ahead, it is ideal for a dinner party.

Serves 4–6

INGREDIENTS
225 g/8 oz/1 cup ricotta cheese
50 g/2 oz/⅓ cup crystallized fruits
60 ml/4 tbsp sweet Marsala
250 ml/8 fl oz/1 cup double (heavy) cream
50 g/2 oz/¼ cup caster (superfine) sugar,
    plus extra to serve
finely grated rind of 1 orange
350 g/12 oz/2 cups fresh raspberries
strips of thinly pared orange rind,
    to decorate

1 Press the ricotta through a sieve into a bowl. Finely chop the crystallized fruits and stir into the ricotta with half of the Marsala.

VARIATION: When soft fruit is not in season you could make this dessert using a topping of crushed macaroons or amaretti biscuits.

2 Put the cream, sugar and finely grated orange rind in another bowl and whip together until the cream is standing in soft peaks.

3 Fold the whipped cream into the ricotta mixture. Spoon into individual glass serving bowls and top with the raspberries. Chill until serving time.

4 Sprinkle with the remaining Marsala and dust the top of each bowl liberally with caster sugar just before serving. Decorate with the thinly pared orange rind.

COOK'S TIP: Buy crystallized fruits in large pieces from a good delicatessen. Tubs of chopped candied peel are too tough to eat raw, and should only be used for baking purposes.

Index

This edition is published by Lorenz Books, an imprint of Anness Publishing Ltd, Blaby Road, Wigston, LE18 4SE

www.lorenzbooks.com; www.annesspublishing.com

If you like the images in this book and would like to investigate using them for publishing, promotions or advertising, please visit our website www.practicalpictures.com for more information.

Publisher: Joanna Lorenz
Editor: Valerie Ferguson & Helen Sudell
Series Designer: Bobbie Colgate Stone
Designer: Andrew Heath
Production Controller: Steve Lang

Recipes contributed by: Catherine Atkinson, Angela Boggiano, Kit Chan, Carole Clements, Roz Denny, Patrizia Diemling, Matthew Drennan, Christine France, Silvano Franco, Shirley Gill, Shehzad Husain, Christine Ingram, Sue Maggs, Annie Nichols, Jenny Stacey, Steven Wheeler, Elizabeth Wolf-Cohen, Jeni Wright.

Photography: William Adams-Lingwood, Karl Adamson, Edward Allwright, James Duncan, Amanda Heywood, Ferguson Hill, Janine Hosegood, Don Last, Peter Reilly, Michael Michaels, Patrick McLeavy, Thomas Odulate.

A CIP catalogue record for this book is available from the British Library

COOK'S NOTES

Bracketed terms are intended for American readers.

For all recipes, quantities are given in both metric and imperial measures and, where appropriate, in standard cups and spoons. Follow one set of measures, but not a mixture, because they are not interchangeable.

Standard spoon and cup measures are level. 1 tsp = 5ml, 1 tbsp = 15ml, 1 cup = 250ml/8fl oz. Australian standard tablespoons are 20ml. Australian readers should use 3 tsp in place of 1 tbsp for measuring small quantities.

American pints are 16fl oz/2 cups. American readers should use 20fl oz/2.5 cups in place of 1 pint when measuring liquids.

Electric oven temperatures in this book are for conventional ovens. When using a fan oven, the temperature will probably need to be reduced by about 10–20°C/20–40°F. Since ovens vary, you should check with your manufacturer's instruction book for guidance.

Medium (US large) eggs are used unless otherwise stated.

PUBLISHER'S NOTE: